Contents

Foreword by Professor Simc

Introduction

Foreword

I am delighted to be writing the foreword to such well-researched and informative book. I have worked at the Royal Botanic Gardens, Kew now for 38 years, having been employed as a senior scientist in the Jodrell laboratory, as Keeper of the Herbarium and more recently as the Head of Strategic Projects in the Directorate.

I have also known Frank Pagnamenta for many years and see him as a man of extraordinary talents and in this book he combines a fluid style of writing with a keen eye for detail. It is fascinating to note his distant relationship to his subjects and the timely production of the book in Kew's 250th year.

William Aiton was an educated, highly skilled gardener from Scotland where he had apparently learned those gardening skills. It is remarkable that Aiton had walked from Scotland to London with little money and his friend Robert Hunter and had managed to find a job at the Chelsea Physic Garden, an ideal placement for his treasured post at Kew. Robert Hunter, whose career was to be in the wine trade, eventually bought a house on Kew Green, and in 1853 that house was to provide the initial location of what is now the most significant botanical Library and Herbarium in the world.

Those who know the Royal Botanic Gardens well will be familiar with the fact that William Aiton was engaged by Princess Augusta to develop her nine-acre physic garden at Kew where the first specific botanical collections were to be grown. William Aiton's appointment in 1759 is considered to be the first year of Kew's existence.

Both William, the father, and then William Townsend, the son, were considered by Kings to be most accomplished horticulturists. They rubbed shoulders with the aristocracy of the day and with the senior scientists and were themselves eminently able and would now be considered accomplished horticultural botanists in their own right.

THE AITONS:
GARDENERS TO THEIR MAJESTIES

by Frank Pagnamenta

With a Foreword by Professor Simon Owens of the
Royal Botanic Gardens, Kew

Richmond Local History Society 2009

ISBN 978-0-9550717-5-1

First Edition

Printed in Great Britain by Kall Kwik,
London Road, Twickenham

A short resumé of the Aitons can be found on the Kew website at http://www.kew.org/heritage/people/aiton.html.

In my time as Keeper of the Herbarium, I had the pleasure of being looked down on by both William Aiton and his wife, Elizabeth. Elizabeth's expression, however, appears to be that of someone who is none too pleased! These small oil portraits, one showing William Aiton holding the plant Aitonia, named after him, remain in the Keeper's room and are believed to be by the sporting and portrait painter Edmund Bristow (1787-1876). Frank Pagnamenta points out that the portrait attributed to John Zoffany is probably not at Kew.

The fate of the Aiton archives is one which leaves me with mixed emotions of sadness and vexation. How much more would we know if those archives still existed and had Frank Pagnamenta been able to pore over the collection of private and professional papers. John Townsend Aiton, William Townsend's brother, was a serious collector of art and artefacts, and it seems completely out of character to destroy what must have included a wealth of historical and horticultural information. Perhaps there were too many skeletons for John's liking, though one can only speculate, as the reasons have been lost in the dusts of time.

Kew has recently established a William Aiton Medal in its 250th Anniversary to recognise exceptional service to Kew, a recognition that would certainly have been bestowed upon the man himself. The medal will be awarded annually.

Dr Simon Owens
Royal Botanic Gardens, Kew
November 2009

Introduction

I first came across William Aiton in 1994, sixteen years ago, when I moved to Richmond from Worcestershire. I soon came to know the Royal Botanic Gardens and I read of the key role in their history played by the Aitons. One of my wife's great-grandparents had had the name Aiton and among family papers was a certificate of birth in 1782 of Hugh Aiton from Carnwath. I saw that William Aiton was also a Scot from Carnwath and I was curious to discover if there was any connection.

As little had been published about William Aiton, I began to make my own enquiries. I found that Hugh was William's second cousin once removed. Their two families had neighbouring farms in Carnwath. Hugh came down from Carnwath to Richmond, was married in Isleworth and had a son, called John, who became a master gardener on large estates.

By this time I had developed an interest in William Aiton himself. I visited places connected with him and se arched such records as I could find. David Blomfield, then editor of the journal of the Richmond Local History Society, thought my enquiries would be of interest to the Society and with his encouragement and help I wrote the series of three articles headed 'The Aitons – Gardeners to their Majesties', for the Society's journal in 1997, 1998, and 1999.

This was my first ever publication and I expected it to be my last. But Dr David Blomfield, now Chairman of the Society, asked if I would be prepared, using these articles as a basis, to produce a booklet on the Aitons for publication to mark the 250th anniversary of William Aiton's engagement in 1759 as the first botanic gardener at Kew, a year now celebrated as the date of birth of the Royal Botanic Gardens. My first reaction, being aged 99, was to say no; however Dr Blomfield offered his help and with further editorial help from Judith Church we have together converted the articles, with a few changes and minor additions, into this publication.

C.F.Pagnamenta, OBE, FCA

Chapter 1: Scottish Roots

The foundation of Kew Gardens is commonly dated from 1759. There were fine gardens on the site for at least a hundred years before this date, but it was in 1759 that the royal accounts first contained a specific separate reference to the costs of the 'Physic Garden', and it was in 1759 that a young Scottish gardener was appointed to have charge of the garden. This gardener was William Aiton, and for the next eighty-two years he and then his son, William Townsend Aiton, were to have the prime responsibility for maintaining and developing the royal gardens at Kew into what we now know as the Royal Botanic Gardens.

In 1759 the Kew gardens were in the grounds of the White House (later to be the first Kew Palace) and were owned by Augusta, Princess of Wales. It was her interest in gardening, shared with her husband Frederick Prince of Wales, and after his death in 1751 supported by the Earl of Bute, that led Augusta to establish her Physic Garden. Bute was a keen botanist, filling his own garden at Kenwood House on Hampstead Heath with exotics. He was a close friend of the Prince and Princess of Wales, and later acted as 'finishing tutor' to their son, later George III.

From his arrival in Kew in 1759 in the reign of George II, through the reigns of George III, George IV, and William IV, to the early years of the reign of Queen Victoria, William Aiton and his two sons had at times charge of royal gardens at Kew, Richmond, Windsor, Buckingham House, Carlton House, and St James's and Kensington Palaces. They clearly had an immense influence on how these gardens were developed, but sadly their professional gardening correspondence and family papers were burnt by William Aiton's younger son John, when they came to him on his brother's death in 1849. It has therefore been necessary to rely on the letters and writings of others, the occasional archive, particularly the Royal Archives and the Duchy of Cornwall Archives, and public records of one kind and another. I acknowledge with thanks the help of all I have consulted, particularly the Royal Botanic Gardens Library.

The family background has by good fortune been provided by an earlier enquiry by another William Aiton, ex-Sheriff Substitute in Hamilton, Lanarkshire. He published in 1830 'An Inquiry into the Origin, Pedigree and History of the Family, or Clan, of Aitons in Scotland'. Sheriff Aiton's first concern was to trace the descent of the Aiton Clan from Yvo Vescey, who held high rank in the army of William of Normandy in 1066, but he went on to comment quite fully on the Aiton families in Scotland in the 17th and 18th centuries and up to his own time. This source, with corroboration and corrections from elsewhere, appears to establish the immediate family background with a fair degree of certainty.[1]

At the beginning of the eighteenth century, there were two related Aiton families in Carnwath, a small agricultural parish in Lanarkshire. They managed the farms of Hillhouse and Boghall on the Westshields estate of Sir William Denholm, a member of the Scottish Parliament. Their unpretentious farmhouses are still there today, with fine views over the rather bleak countryside to the hills in the far distance. John Aiton, William's father, was farming at Boghall when his eldest son, also John, was born in 1723.

After Sir William's death, his widow married Daniel Campbell of Shawfield as his second wife. Daniel Campbell (1672-1753) was a colourful character of considerable influence. A wealthy Glasgow merchant, he was closely connected with the Duke of Argyll. He was collector of customs at Port Glasgow, a member of the Scottish Parliament, and a commissioner for the union of Scotland and England. He was popularly best known in connection with the riots at Glasgow against the malt tax in 1725, when the fine house he had built at Shawfield on the outskirts of the city was burnt down by the mob, because of his supposed part in promoting the tax. By a vote of the House of Commons he was awarded £6,080 compensation, which the Government recovered from Glasgow whose magistrates were supposed to have connived at the riots. Campbell used the money to buy the islands of Islay and Jura.

Campbell's seat at Woodhall near Glasgow was a considerable property, and it seems that John Aiton senior was so highly regarded by the new

Lady Campbell that she persuaded him to move and manage the farming on the estate. His next two children were born at Woodhall and christened at the local parish church at Bothwell – James in January 1727, and William, who was to become the King's gardener at Kew, in April 1733.

The entry in the Bothwell register, which is the true beginning of this story, reads: 'Aiton. William son lawful to John Aiton in Woodhall and Jean Weir his spouse born the 16th April and baptised the 29th of the month in the Church of Bothwell. 1733.' (All published information, including his tombstone, assumes 1731 as the year of William's birth. A likely explanation is that when he first came to London seeking work he overstated his age, and was stuck with his claim for the rest of his life and beyond.) It was probably on Campbell's estate that he received his training. His eldest brother, John, would succeed their father, and be Factor to Campbell.

At the age of twenty-one, William Aiton came south to seek his fortune, following, or perhaps leading, the flood of Scottish gardeners who crossed the border in the 18th century looking for employment in England or further afield. They were evidently educated and highly skilled and consequently in demand. Among the emigrants according to ex-Sheriff Aiton were four other Aitons, including William's brother James, who was employed by a family in Lancashire. Another John Aiton from Carnwath was highly regarded in England and was then recruited by Jeremy Bentham to work with his brother Samuel on Potemkin's estate in Belorussia in the 1780s; later he may have been among a number of Scottish gardeners employed by Catherine the Great on her many projects. Yet another was Hugh Aiton, born in Carnwath in 1782, and married in Isleworth, Middlesex, in 1810. His son John was christened at St Mary Magdalene, Richmond, in January 1811, and also trained as a gardener, possibly under his cousin, William Townsend Aiton. In 1851 this son was head gardener to the Earl of Stamford, employing 35 men and boys at Enville, where he died in 1860.

William Aiton came to London in 1754 and the story is that he and his friend Robert Hunter had walked from Scotland with very little money. Aiton was somehow introduced to Philip Miller, another Scot, at the Physic Garden, Chelsea, where he spent four or five useful years before being recommended to take charge of Princess Augusta's Physic Garden at Kew. His friend Robert Hunter is said to have come with a letter of introduction to a wine merchant in the city, where he established a successful career. The two were to keep in touch over the years, Hunter later buying a house on Kew Green (now part of the Herbarium of the Botanic Gardens).

Aiton's recommendation to Kew is variously attributed to Philip Miller, or Lord Bute, or the incumbent gardener, John Haverfield; it is quite likely that they all had a hand in it, and possibly Campbell's relationship to the Duke of Argyll, Bute's uncle, counted in his favour. Argyll had himself established a fine garden and arboretum nearby in Whitton.

The household accounts of Augusta, Dowager Princess of Wales, show that not long before William Aiton was first at Kew, John Haverfield had taken over as Head Gardener following the death of Robert Greening. Initially, before his contract was established, John Haverfield submitted detailed claims for his expenses and there is no mention of the Physic Garden or Aiton at that stage.[2] The Physic Garden first appears in October 1759 when a contract figure payable to Haverfield was established 'for ordering and cultivating Her Royal Highness's gardens at Kew' at the same fee as Greening i.e. £700 p.a., with an extra £50 p.a. for the 'Physic Garden'.

It is generally said that William Aiton took charge of the Physic Garden in 1759, and it is possible that he was then engaged at a salary of £50 to assist Haverfield, providing the experience of exotics which Haverfield lacked. A later gardener, John Smith, wrote a history of the Gardens in which he confidently states that Aiton was appointed in 1759, 'superintendent of the newly commissioned physic/botanic/garden, which he laid out and planted'.[3] However, it is not until in January 1763 that William Aiton appears in the household accounts in his own name, and from then on is paid £120 p.a. for 'cultivating and keeping in order our Physic Garden'. At the same time John Haverfield is paid £700 p.a. 'for cultivating and keeping in order our Pleasure Grounds and Orangery, Kitchen Garden and Melon Ground at Kew', with no mention of the Physic Garden in relation to Haverfield.[4] This state of affairs continued until the death of her Royal Highness on 8 February 1772, except that from July 1764 Aiton was paid an extra 9s. per week for a labourer.

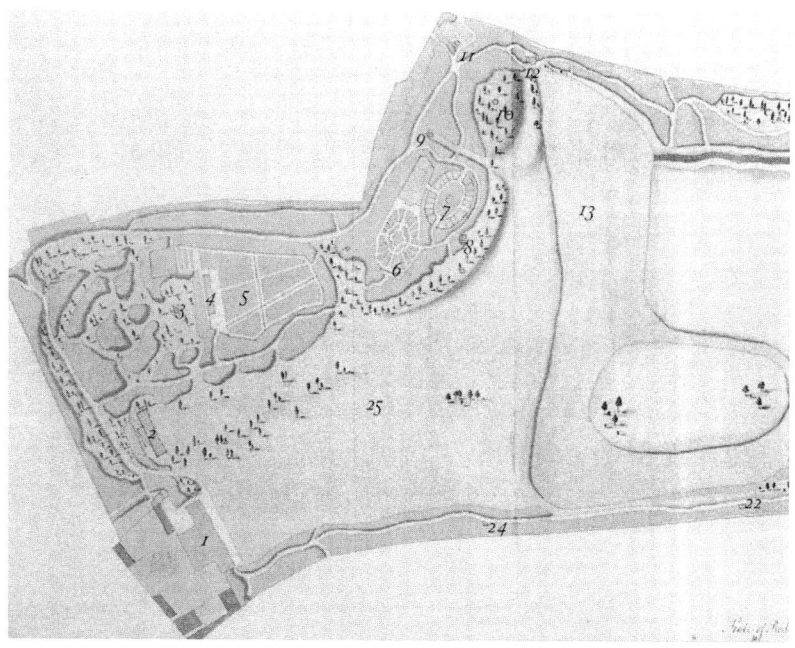

This detail from a 1763 plan of Princess Augusta's garden, adapted by Ray Desmond for his *Kew: the History of the Royal Botanic Gardens,* indicates the nine acres occupied by the Physic Garden (no.5) and Arboretum (no.3). The Orangery is no 2. (Map courtesy British Library)

The years 1759 to 1762 would have established Aiton's standing, leading to his appointment in charge of the Physic Garden in his own right in January 1763, but it is possible that his marriage about that time was the occasion for this preferment by a benevolent and satisfied employer. No record of his marriage has

11

been found, but since his first child Elizabeth Townsend Aiton was born in 1764 it is fair to assume that he was married between 1760 and 1763, and that his wife came from Kew or Chelsea or thereabouts. We know from the inscription on her tombstone that she was born in 1740, and from the registers of St Luke's, Chelsea, that an Elizabeth Townsend was christened there in 1740. The coincidence of name, date and place makes it a reasonable assumption that she became Mrs Aiton.

We also know that a small house in the royal gardens near Kew Green was allotted to William Aiton in about 1760, as his son, in a letter written in 1840, said it had been the family home for 'eighty years'. (Much enlarged in 1787, it now overlooks the traffic lights at the junction of the Kew and Mortlake Roads.) Here the Aitons brought up their two sons, William (born 1766) and John (1777), and four daughters, Elizabeth (1764), the twins Sarah and Jane (1768) and Ann Augusta (1781). All were given the second name Townsend, seemingly to maintain Mrs Aiton's maiden name.

In the nine years from Aiton's appointment in charge in 1763 until the death of Augusta Dowager Princess of Wales in 1772, life must have been very full with the rising reputation of the Gardens in his care, and his growing family. Apart from the general cultivation of the nine-acre Physic Garden and arboretum, he would have been busy with a flow of exotic plants, many coming as gifts, others from overseas as the result of Bute's efforts to collect for the Princess's garden the best in the world. Ray Desmond, in his magisterial history of the Royal Botanic Gardens, records this compliment paid to Aiton by a famously generous donor, John Ellis. 'I have sent Mr Aiton, her Royal Highness the Princess Dowager of Wales's Botanic Gard'ner at Kew, a parcel of seeds and don't doubt but he will raise them; as he is a perfect master of his business.'[5] New 'stoves' (heated greenhouses) gave Aiton the conditions necessary for their care. After the Duke of Argyll's death in 1761 Bute brought many unusual plants and trees from the Argyll garden in Whitton to be re-established at Kew, some of which survive to this day, probably where Aiton put them in Kew's arboretum.[6]

Kew's *Sophora Japonica,* a living monument to Aiton's arboretum (Photo courtesy Julian Wolfreys)

It is not easy to recognise the guiding hand at this time. All would have been under the eye of Augusta, though in the years immediately before her death she was herself less and less at Kew. Lord Bute, as Prime Minister from 1762 to 1763, must perforce have been able to give less time to Kew than in the past, though he still had his house on Kew Green. After he ceased to be Prime Minister, and by the time he went abroad for his health for several years in 1769, we are told that Bute 'no longer had any influence at Kew'.[7] We know that John Hill, who was in charge of the Gardens at Kensington, was required to make regular visits to Kew, publishing his *Hortus Kewensis* in 1768 with a second edition in 1769, but it is unlikely that he had authority over Aiton.[8] The conclusion is that Aiton must have been quietly developing the garden on his own initiative.

Almost certainly, however, Joseph Banks, who was a close friend and confidant of the King, was finding time to visit Kew between his ventures to Newfoundland, the South Seas and Australia with Cook in the *Endeavour,* and then to Iceland. In Kew, he would have met Aiton, providing inspiration and encouragement. A charismatic character, Banks was ten years Aiton's junior, very wealthy by inheritance, with a deep interest in botany, extremely able, genial, enthusiastic, adventurous, with sound judgment. He then had no official position at Court, nor in Kew, but it was the effect of his influence that would now carry the Garden forward.

13

Chapter 2: Gardener to the King

After Princess Augusta died in February 1772, her son George III moved into the White House at Kew, and from then on took a considerable interest in the garden. Banks now became the unofficial Honorary but very involved Director, though Aiton retained control of the garden operation throughout. Distinguished visitors were to be dealt with, many from overseas and other botanical gardens in Britain; so were correspondence and exchange of plants and seeds, complicated arrangements for collection and delivery, and Customs and other problems with plants after a long sea voyage. He was busy too with his own *Hortus Kewensis*.

Clearly, Banks and Aiton developed a mutual regard. This glows through their references to each other and, going beyond a simple professional relationship, would later help Aiton's widow secure a pension. However, in all Sir Joseph Banks's voluminous published correspondence only one letter from William Aiton is mentioned: '(1780 May 20): Informs B. that *Cornus florida* is in flower in Lady Galloway's garden in Sion Lane; "it is well worth a persons going a hundred miles to see it."'[9] This evidently was something worth writing about!

In 1783 William Aiton was appointed chief gardener of the Kitchen and Pleasure Gardens at Kew, in addition to the Botanic Garden, and he benefited from a noticeable increase in income. The Haverfields, whom he replaced, retained responsibility for the contiguous royal 'Richmond Gardens' which were divided from the 'Kew Gardens' by Love Lane. (The line of Love Lane is marked in the present gardens by the Holly Walk.) This was the beginning of the end of the dominance of the Haverfields in the royal gardens. In 1785 the closure of Love Lane was authorised by Act of Parliament, and slowly over the coming years the two gardens began to reflect their single ownership.

Soon after Aiton was given care of all the gardens at Kew, orders were given on the King's instructions for the gardener's house to be enlarged. (Its small size must have been a problem as his family grew.) A letter from Sir Francis Drake, Master of the Household, to the Lords Commissioners of the Treasury in June 1786 implies that the Treasury had questioned the expense, as he explains that it 'is really such a building as never hardly to have deserved the name of a dwelling house'.[10]

In July Sir William Chambers, Controller of Works at Kew and the King's architect, wrote saying, '...I have caused a Survey to be made of the [gardener's house at Kew] and also Plans of the Alterations and Additions necessary, to render it convenient for the Master Gardeners Family...'; he estimated the cost at £855 7s.[11] On 21 July a Treasury Warrant authorised the work to be 'done in a substantial and workmanlike Manner'.[12] It was completed in June 1787 at a cost of £966 19 10½. The house still stands, now as no.199 Kew Road. Under the name of Descanso House, it is the address of the Botanic Gardens Conservation International.

Descanso House

Aiton was clearly a supreme master of his profession in the propagation and care of plants from every climate. He also must have been an able judge and manager of men. It fell to him to recommend gardeners or botanists sent over the world in that exciting age of discovery to seek out new plants and bring them home to His Majesty's garden, where he would take care of them. He also had the considerable task of administering their employment.

He was not an academic but he numbered many learned men among his friends and they worked happily with him. His *magnum opus*, and his only publication, was his *Hortus Kewensis*, or *Catalogue of Plants cultivated in the Royal Botanic Gardens at Kew*, published in 1789 in three volumes with 13 coloured engravings. It sold out in two years. He dedicated the work to George III, and in so doing said that the work had 'cost him a large portion of the leisure allowed by the daily duties of his station, during more than sixteen years'.

Aiton acknowledged that his *Hortus Kewensis* would not have been possible without 'the assistance of men more learned' than himself, though there has been criticism that he did not refer to them by name and more effusively. It seems to have been a good example of co-operation between disciplines. Aiton, the practical man, planned the book, listing the plants, adding dates of introduction to British gardens, distinguishing between trees, shrubs and herbaceous plants, whether annual, hardy or tender, and their flowering periods. Two scientists, Dr Solander and Dr Dryander, both from Sweden and on Banks's staff, provided the taxonomic classification, Latin names and descriptions and editing. It was this combination of the scientific and the practical that made the publication outstanding.

Aiton was a man of remarkable character. It is a tragedy that his younger son burnt his father's and brother's papers, but this, together with the fact that none of the six children married, though they all lived to a good age, suggests an unusual family. As a Scot and a Presbyterian, William Aiton was not a regular member of the congregation at St Anne's on Kew Green, and the Aitons do not appear to have been in what might be called 'Kew

Society', which would then have centred on the church and the Vestry, and have been dominated to some degree by the Haverfields who would have regarded themselves as the rightful Kew Gardeners.

One of his neighbours, however, was clearly a close friend. This was the distinguished court painter Johann Zoffany (1733-1810) who had a house in Chiswick, at Strand-on-the-Green. Zoffany painted a portrait of Aiton, on which Aiton clearly set great store, as he bequeathed it in his will with specific instruction to his successors:

> to my dear Wife Eliza Aiton my picture painted by my friend Zoffany and after her decease I do request it may go to my Eldest Child who shall be living at that time of her decease and it is my wish that after the death of such Son or Daughter the next eldest of my dear Children shall have the Right to Claim it namely my picture and so on by rotation so long as any of my children are living.

There is now some confusion over this picture. There are two existing portraits of William Aiton at Kew. The first is a delightful small picture, in which he is seen holding *Aitonia*, named after him by C.P.P.Thunberg.[13] The second is a larger more impressive portrait, now appropriately in Aiton House, the new administration block and micro-propagation laboratory. The latter seems to be a not very good copy of the smaller portrait, and could have been painted after Aiton's death, perhaps at the same time as the portrait of Mrs Aiton, which is attributed to E.Bristow (1787-1876). There is a third portrait in the form of a miniature by the royal miniaturist George Engleheart, which is now in a private collection.

We know that after the death of his youngest child, a portrait of Aiton was sent to the then Director of the Gardens, Sir William Hooker, and it has been assumed that it was the Zoffany portrait. However, experts at the National Portrait Gallery are inclined to the view that neither of the pictures at Kew was painted by Zoffany. Their provenance and the whereabouts of the Zoffany portrait are at this time a mystery.

William Aiton

This portrait – once believed to be by Aiton's friend Johann Zoffany –
is reproduced by kind permission of the Royal Botanic Gardens.

Elizabeth Aiton

This portrait, by E.Bristow, is reproduced by kind permission of the
Royal Botanic Gardens.

Aiton died 'in harness' on 2 February 1793 at the relatively young age of 59, thirty years after taking personal charge of the Physic Garden which had under his care established a worldwide reputation. At his funeral at St Anne's, Kew Green, 'his pall was supported by Sir Joseph Banks, the Rev. Dr Goodenough, Mr Dryander, Dr Pitcairn, Mr Dundas of Richmond, and Mr Zoffani.'[14] Banks, Dryander, and Zoffany have already been mentioned. Two of the others were distinguished medical men who attended the King – Mr Dundas, who later became Sir David Dundas, Bart, and an honorary member of the Royal College of Surgeons, and Dr David Pitcairn, physician to St Bartholomew's Hospital, of which the King was patron. They probably attended Aiton in his last illness. Dr Goodenough, later Bishop of Carlisle, at that time ran a well-established school in Ealing for 'the sons of noblemen and gentlemen of position'. He was a keen botanist, being one of the founders, the first treasurer, and a vice-president of the Linnean Society, as well as vice-president of the Royal Society. He is credited with writing, under the name of *Kewensis,* an obituary of Aiton to which the *Gentleman's Magazine* of 6 May 1793 unusually devoted two pages.

William Aiton was buried in a family vault in St Anne's churchyard, where he would be followed over the years by his wife and all his six children. His funeral sermon, however, was preached not at St Anne's but at Brentford fifteen days after his death – not so strange when one notes that his name is among the trustees who were parties to the purchase of land for the Brentford Presbyterian chapel in 1792. It was preached by the Rev.W.Smith of Camberwell, a graduate of Edinburgh University and educated in Aberdeen, evidently an old friend. It was published by Mr Robert Gray of Richmond, presumably another friend of the Aitons. In the sermon he is described as 'a true Christian ... most liberal in his sentiments and conduct with regard to the established Church of this country... When he could not conveniently get to a meeting house, he cordially joined in the service of the Church of England'. Aiton is then quoted as saying: 'We have each but one faith and one hope – we differ only in the little unessential modes and ceremonies – good men there undoubtedly are in both sects, and ere long we must worship

20

together in the same place — Is it not to be desired then that we should sometimes assemble together here below?'

Modern sentiments indeed!

Aiton's character is perhaps epitomised in a letter written a month after his death from the Marchioness of Rockingham to J.E.Smith, President of the Linnean Society:

> I little thought five years ago, that I could have felt so much concern for the death of Mr Aiton; but I had not seen him then, and only looked on him as the Kew gardener: but the single quarter of an hour that he was with me here occasioned an instantaneous conversion. I was quite charmed with the plainness of his manners without a grain of that pomposity one might have expected; but on the contrary, quite pleasant and communicative in his profession: in short, he took my fancy so much that I cannot help feeling infinite regret that so great and good a man in his line should be no more.'[15]

There is also the account by Colonel Greville, George III's equerry, of an episode at Kew on 11 February 1789, when the King was recovering from his first period of temporary insanity with unhappy memories of the treatments prescribed by Dr Willis:

> HMy's second walk was in the Exotic Garden where he saw Mr Eaton [sic] his Botanic Gardener — who was talking to Dr Willis. The King overheard his promise to make up a basket of exotic plants for the doctor one of these days; on hearing this, He added, 'Get another basket Eaton at the same time, & pack the doctor in it, and send him off at the same time.[16]

Richard Mabey in *The Flowering of Kew* gives us another picture:

> The pilgrimage which best illustrates the magnetism and social mix of Kew in its early years was that made by William Cobbett, farmer's son turned radical MP. Cobbett

walked to Kew from Farnham in 1774 when he was just eleven, climbed the wall and fell asleep over a copy of Swift's *A Tale of a Tub*. The next morning he went off to see the head gardener, William Aiton, and was given a job. He retained a lifelong affection for Kew, and a distinct memory of young Prince William and his brothers laughing at his rustic clothes as he was 'sweeping the grass plot at the foot of the Pagoda.'[17]

Shortly after he died, his wife wrote to Banks asking for support in securing a pension:

Sir, The Recollection of so many years past intimacy and friendship that subsisted without interruption, between you and my late Affectionate and to me ever to be lamented Husband and the many acts of kindness, civility and friendship, he and his Family have experienced from you induces me at this time to solicit your Attention and to represent the embarrassment I labour under... Duty and Affection to my Family Sir impels me to disclose to you the narrow circumstances I find myself left in, with four Daughters, depending upon me; yet with heart felt Gratitude for His Majesty's great goodness and Benevolence in appointing my Eldest Son to succeed his Father, whose truly Filial Affection, and fraternal Disposition, is a source of much comfort to all the Family; he likewise has the whole charge of Learning his Brother the Profession, and preparing him to be an Useful Member of Society, which gives my Mind great relief and satisfaction.

But for near twenty years after our Marriage we had to struggle with difficulties, in supporting a Decent appearance, in bringing up our Children and giving them Education; for it is only since the addition of the whole Gardens at Kew being given to my late Husband, that he found himself in easy Circumstances, and beginning to make Provision for his Family, when the will of Heaven took from me the best of husbands, and from my Dear

22

Children the Kindest and most Affectionate of Fathers ...

I need not inform you Sir, who knew him so well of his Temperance, Sobriety and Oeconomy, through Life, yet with all these, and every Domestic Assistance, he has not left a Sufficiency, wherewith to maintain his Family, in that state of Decency and Comfort which appeared in his Life time, whenever they come to be separated from my Sons Habitation... So truly sensible was my late Husband of this, that he importun'd me on his Death Bed to lay my Situation by Petition at his Majesty's feet; and if possible, through the medium and friendship of Sir Joseph Banks. Oh Sir, permit me then to request this singular Act of friendship from you; for I have neither in myself Resolution, nor Spirits, to support me in approaching his Majesty's Presence, on this trying Occasion. I have ventured herewith to inclose a Petition to his Majesty, tho' inadequately worded like this; I rely on your Candour, and leave to your judgment, friendship, and Discretion to make the best use of them.

In the grateful fullness of my heart, I remain, Sir,

Your much Oblig' d & most Humble Serv't,

Kew, July 29th 1793.   Elizabeth Aiton.

This letter is from the Royal Archives. It was apparently submitted to the King by Banks. Mrs Aiton received a Pension from the King's Bounty of £150 p.a. until she died in 1825.

Chapter 3: The Son Succeeds

When his father died on 2 February 1793, the day on which war with France was renewed, it was William Townsend Aiton's 27th birthday. Four days later, on the recommendation of Sir Joseph Banks and Sir Francis Drake, Master of the Royal Household, a Royal Warrant was issued, appointing him in his father's place.

As well as being given his father's office as 'The King's Gardener at Kew' he inherited responsibility for his mother, four unmarried sisters and a younger brother, John Townsend Aiton, then 16, who had just left school and started his garden apprenticeship. He also inherited occupation of the house on Kew Road, on the Royal Estate, which the King had rebuilt for his father six years earlier.

His mother died in 1825, and by 1848 all his sisters were also dead; none of them had married and they appear to have spent the whole of their lives in their brother's house. All were interred in the family vault built for their father in the cemetery of St Anne's Church on Kew Green, and are recorded on the handsome tombstone of classical design erected on the plot in the churchyard purchased from the Kew Vestry by their mother on the death of their father.

All the children were born and brought up in the house on Kew Road, and the only light shed on the life they led comes from an anecdote related by Robert Brown, a friend of J.T.Aiton and Librarian to Sir Joseph Banks:

> On one occasion when skating with the youthful Royal Princes, H.M. unexpectedly appeared. William scampered off, but was soon brought back before the King, not however to be reprimanded but to be kindly informed that he was also to have the benefit together with the Princes of the instruction of Mr West in skating, an art in which he became unusually accomplished.[18]

24

The Aiton tomb at St Anne's, Kew Green

William Townsend was educated at Dr Rose's School in Chiswick for six years, going on to Bower House School in Camberwell under the Rev.W.Smith for two and a half years before being apprenticed to his father in Kew. Dr Rose's school had originally been on Kew Green. The Rev.W.Smith, a friend of the family, gave the obituary address at his father's funeral service.

By the time of his father's death, William Townsend Aiton had already gained the confidence of Sir Joseph Banks, Sir Francis Drake, and of the King. He had also, in addition to his education in gardening and botany under his father, studied landscape gardening in which he wished to make a career.

He had undertaken a number of commissions as a landscape gardener, including Heathfield House at Turnham Green for Lord Heathfield, who had been well rewarded as the defender of Gibraltar in 1779-83. He was a frequent visitor to Windsor, perhaps in connection with the Queen's garden at Frogmore. He appears to have designed and overseen the erection of greenhouses for the Royal family at Frogmore and for Lady Jennings Clerke at Holly Grove in Windsor Great Park.[19] He would also be credited in the Linnean Society tribute on his death with landscape or garden design work for the Earl of Chesterfield, Lord Boston, Sir William Ashton, Lord Harrowby, the Earl of Powis, Lord Palmerston, the Hon. E. Greville, Sir F. Drake, Sir H. Strachey, HRH the Duke of Kent, and 'many other noblemen and gentlemen'. His interest in landscape gardening would also lead to his designing in later life the East Terrace at Windsor and working with Nash on the gardens at Buckingham Palace, Brighton Pavilion and St James's. In the 1790s, however, when his father's health was failing, he was increasingly helping in the management of the Kew gardens.

William Townsend began his duties as the King's Royal Gardener in Kew in the same dual employment as his father. He was responsible to the Lord Steward, under contract for the Kitchen and Pleasure Gardens at Kew and Richmond. He was responsible to His Majesty directly 'by custom and practice' for the Botanic Garden through the Master of the Household, and paid from the Privy Purse.

The distinction may seem more apparent than real, but it seems likely that it was real in Aiton's mind. He worked with Sir Joseph Banks, and to great effect, on the Botanic Garden but Banks probably had little to do with the kitchen, flower, and pleasure gardens from which Aiton derived most of his income and which occupied most of his gardeners.

When he was first appointed, the Botanic Garden would have been his main concern. In August 1793, soon after he took over, HMS *Providence* docked at Deptford with the largest single dispatch ever made to Kew.[20] *Providence* had been accompanied by *Assistant,* and their cargo included '1283 plants from Tahiti, Tasmania, New Guinea, Timor, St Vincent and Jamaica'. This dispatch was followed by a succession of collections of new plants from overseas needing Aiton's special skills. In May 1796, for instance, HMS *Royal Admiral* arrived from Calcutta with the largest presentation of plants since the *Providence.*[21] Some years later, on 16 March 1804, £210 was paid for 'Cayenne Plants' to the captain of a vessel who had taken them from a French prize.[22]

In 1794, following the death of Thomas Methold (at one time churchwarden of Kew), the King purchased his garden of over three acres, and added it to the Royal garden under Aiton's care.[23] On the following day, John Haverfield was instructed to 'close the kitchen garden at Richmond as soon as the present crops are off'.[24]

This resulted in a loss of income to Haverfield, who in a letter to the Lord Steward the following May asked for compensation. Haverfield was subsequently placed on the Bounty List for a pension of £250 p.a.[25] Aiton was then given a contract dated 11 December 1795 'for the Kitchen, Pleasure and Flower Gardens at Kew and Richmond' at a fixed fee of £1878 1s 6d p.a. plus head money.

The contract was extremely detailed as for all the Royal Gardens: the Abstract alone ran to ten pages.[26] It gave Aiton care of:

Kitchen Gardens:	12 acres at £40 per acre
Fine Keeping at Richmond and Kew:	65 acres at £10 per acre
Lawn Keeping at Kew and Richmond:	110 acres at £3 per acre
Lawrels at the bottom of the Pit at Richmond:	2 acres at £5 per acre
Canal at Kew:	7 acres at £1 per acre
Hot Houses and for forcing Fruits	
Pheasant Pens	
Water Engine at Kew	
Filling the Ice House	

'Fine Keeping' required mowing – which must have been with scythe – and sweeping every fortnight, or more often in summer. The Lawns, 'appointed to be fed with His Majesty's sheep', had to be mowed four times a year and brushed, harrowed and rolled at least eight times. Waters were to be kept clean and he must take care of the fish. Detailed requirements were issued for flower beds, shrubs, hot houses, trees, care of paths and disposal of produce. The Water Engine was to be regularly worked with two horses throughout the summer. All costs, including labour, horses, plants, manure etc. were to be met by Aiton, who was not however responsible for maintenance of the buildings. All was subject to two months notice on failure to comply with contract terms, and Aiton bound himself to due performance in a penalty of £1000. In addition he had charge of the Botanic Garden, which is not mentioned in the contract but must have required his personal attention.

Aiton was now sufficiently established to dedicate a collection of prints of Kew heathers, mainly from South Africa, by Francis Bauer, to Queen Charlotte, wife of George III. 'No event,' he wrote, 'so materially tended to increase the Royal Collection, as that decided preference which our most Gracious Queen has of late condescended to bestow upon the science of botany.'[27]

In May 1801 the King addressed a paper to Mr Henry Strachey, the new Master of the Household, with the following introduction: 'The King during his stay at Kew, has frequently examined the Kitchen Garden, and very much approves of Mr Aiton's manner of conducting it, besides being much pleased with his Candid Manner of confessing that all Mr Strachey's Regulations, as to the manner of settling the Contracts, are perfectly just.' He went on to express the wish that all the Gardens be placed under the direction of Mr Strachey including the Botanic Garden, and the kitchen gardens of Windsor and Great Lodge jointly between William and John Aiton, and that 'for greater accuracy' all deliveries for the use of the Kitchens be valued at the market price and 'consequently stand against the expense of cultivating the Gardens' and the surplus sold and accounted for to Mr Strachey.[28]

From Michaelmas 1801 the expenses of the Botanic Garden, met before most probably from the Privy Purse, were to be paid by the Board of the Green Cloth, the main instrument for organisation and accountancy in the Royal Household under the Lord Steward (so called from the green-covered table at which its business was originally conducted). Aiton was required to submit detailed returns of Garden expenses and also of deliveries. He was paid a salary of £500 p.a. as a Botanic Garden expense, increased to £600 in 1807, on the grounds that 'the many overseas collections received have required an increase in labour' and enclosing William McNab's accounts.[29] (McNab was then a foreman at Kew; he would later become Curator of the Royal Botanic Gardens in Edinburgh.)

In 1805, following a change in the dining arrangements at Court with the 'abolition of the Tables of the Maids of Honour and the Chaplains', the Master of the Household (now *Sir* Henry Strachey) wrote to Aiton saying in effect that this must result in a surplus of produce being available for sale and asking for monthly returns of produce sold.[30] This sort of correspondence continued for a number of years both at Kew and Windsor. No 'returns' have been found in the records, but there are year-end letters saying that demand and consumption left nothing for sale, and 'consequently I have no market accounts to deliver'. At about the same time (1806) it was reported to the King that 94 trees had been blown down in a gale, and strict rules were made to cover the handling and sale of the timber.[31] The Household were either doing their conscientious duty or were suspicious; but at no time was any cause for suspicion mentioned.

Aiton seems now to have felt that, with the garden contract handed on to the Board of Green Cloth, he had time for some outside interests. Although his family had not been much involved in Kew society, he had played a minor role in Kew Vestry. In 1797 he was one of twenty-eight leading members of the community to back a resolution that the new Vicar was not entitled to Pew Money as of right, as it had been voted to his predecessor only when the emoluments were very small. The following year he was appointed a Trustee of the Old Charity School Fund and thereafter was often at the Vestry meetings.

William Townsend Aiton

This portrait by L. Poyot is reproduced by kind permission of the Royal Botanic Gardens.

Regardless of pressure of work, he attended when matters arose affecting the Royal Family at Kew: in a sense he acted as go-between. He was certainly there at a dramatic meeting in 1803, with the Duke of Cumberland in the Chair. It had been called, in the face of a threatened French invasion, to make a Public Appeal to form a Kew Volunteer Detachment. The meeting resolved 'that a Committee be formed of the Gentlemen hereafter named, to transact business and adopt such Measures as Circumstances may demand'. The committee was to be chaired by the Duke. Among its eight members was Mr Aiton. A total of 157 Kew residents signed the resolution, including a number of gardeners at Kew, some of whom, like McNab, would distinguish themselves elsewhere in later years.

The Pay List for the Kew Volunteers for the year to 24 December 1804 shows Capt Robt. Tunstall (builder of the second Kew Bridge) in command, supported by Lieut William T. Aiton, and Ensign Robt. G. Kidd, with 66 other ranks.[32] (The invasion threat soon passed; there are no more Pay Lists in the records, and in 1807 the Secretary at War was informed that the Kew Volunteer Legion had been disbanded.) [33]

Later Aiton's attendance became less frequent. He was appointed Overseer of the Poor at the Kew Vestry meeting on 2 April 1804, but by November James Clewley was acting as Overseer on his behalf, and Widden and Davison were appointed in Aiton's place the following year. However, he did appear when matters of especial importance were under discussion, as in 1810 when there were proposals for a free school, in 1813 for warming the church, and in 1817 for an extension of the churchyard, by petition to the Queen as Lady of the Manor.

Despite the invasion threat, 1803 had produced an influx of plants, amongst which 'Guinea plants ... arrived at Kew in three barges' from a French prize *L'Union,* 'intended as a present to Madame Bonaparte, Tallyrant & that company'. Fortunately a new greenhouse which Aiton had pressed for was completed.[34] At this time too he was involved in discussions for the formation of what became the Royal Horticultural Society, being canvassed by William Forsyth, Royal Gardener at Kensington and St James's, who was the prime mover, and he attended the preliminary meeting at Hatchards on 14 March 1804 when the decision to form the society was taken.[35] A month later, both he and his brother John attended the first meeting of the Society as founding members, and subsequently during the year to consider rules and organisation.

31

When William Forsyth died on 25 July 1804 Aiton interceded with the King for his friend William Forsyth Jnr to succeed his father at Kensington and St James's, but His Majesty replied that it was already disposed of. When Aiton arrived home he found that it was he himself who 'in a letter written in the King's own hand was appointed with graciously expressed Royal commendation to fulfil the duties of gardener at Richmond, Kew and Kensington and his brother John that of gardener at Windsor and the Great Park'.[36] His contract followed, covering 'Kitchen, Pleasure and Flower Gardens at Kensington and also His Majesty's Garden at St James Palace', in the whole £1539 17s 3d.[37] The terms of the contract paralleled the Richmond and Kew contract, and brought under his care: 'Kitchen Garden, 12 acres, Greenhouse, Strawberry house, Garden and Lawn at Kensington 146 acres, the St James' Garden, the Bason 7 acres, and the Canal 9 acres'.

Aiton's appointment appears to have been on the King's own initiative without consulting Banks or Aiton. Banks in a letter to Sir James Smith (a distinguished botanist and first President of the Linnean Society) on August 10 wrote that he 'would have had infinite pleasure' in recommending James Donn of the Cambridge Botanic Garden to the King as a proper person to cultivate Kensington Palace Gardens, but H.M. had already appointed Aiton, and further that 'this arrangement is clearly intended to complete the provision which the King intended to made for the two Aitons...so that both brothers will be able to live comfortably'.[38] Consequently William Townsend Aiton now had charge of nearly 400 acres of Royal gardens at Kew, Richmond, Kensington and St James's under precise and demanding obligations as to care and maintenance to a high standard. In addition he had charge of the Botanic Garden, small in area but requiring exceptional skill from the gardener.

He was clearly an administrator of ability as well as having first-class experience as a general and an exotic gardener, and he was able to train or attract and keep able assistants. He was also able to work with and under the direction of Sir Joseph Banks in maintaining and developing the Botanic Garden. Many young men were recruited by him as gardeners who later distinguished themselves in appointments in Great Britain and across the world. It was his custom to put them to train initially in some other garden under his care, bringing them to Kew only when they had proved themselves – as happened to John Smith, a famous Kew gardener who was to become Curator under Hooker. Smith was at Kensington for two years, before going on to Kew.

In 1805 the Duke of Kent had returned after many years overseas to establish a new home at Castle Hill, near Ealing. It would be said in the Linnean Society Obituary Address on Aiton's death that Aiton had kept up a confidential correspondence with the Duke, and that he had designed a garden for him. This may well have been at Castle Hill. No correspondence survives.

After George III's last visit to Kew in January 1806, prior to his long retirement at Windsor, Kew began to lose its prime importance as a Royal Residence but it kept its vigour as a Botanic Garden thanks largely to the interest of Sir Joseph Banks. An instance of the involvement of Banks at Kew appears in Aiton's letter to Colonel W.Price at Frogmore in November 1807, which was sent along with two black swans from New South Wales, which Banks had instructed him to send accompanied by a 'dwarf old man tree reputed to be over 100 years old' given to the Queen by a rich Chinese merchant as an example of an art peculiar to the Chinese.[39]

As well as being responsible for Kew and Richmond, Aiton was now supervising the gardens at Kensington and St James's which were each under the immediate care of a competent foreman. Quite properly he seems to have intervened only when things went wrong. In 1810, for instance, he had to write to the Board of Green Cloth pointing out that a stone fence or posts and chain had not, as requested, been placed in front of Kensington Palace with the result that the lawns and beds were being ruined by carriages 'driving over the walks and lawns to the great injury of the Royal Gardens ... when the Princess has her parties'.[40] On another occasion he wrote to the Surveyor General regarding the flooding of the Hot Houses by spring water in winter: new drains were needed.[41]

At Kensington a new ten-acre kitchen garden was established over the years 1813-1815 by command of the Prince Regent, and by contract from the Treasury seven new hot houses were built. This increased the garden contract by some £900, raising the annual amount for Aiton's keeping these Gardens to £2,869.[42] At the same time he was involved with the Gardens at Brighton where expenses were settled through him in 1814.[43]

With the King's continuing illness, the Prince of Wales had taken the Oath as Prince Regent on 5 February 1811, with little apparent effect on Aiton except that on 6 July 1812 he was by Warrant (from the Prince Regent) appointed to the place of Gardener in Ordinary at Carlton House.[44] He also became involved with alterations to the Gardens at Cranbourne Lodge, in Windsor, where a new forcing house was to be built 'agreeably to Mr Aiton's requisition'.[45]

From 1803 onwards Aiton had also been engaged, with the encouragement of Sir Joseph Banks, in revising his father's famous Kew Catalogue, his *Hortus Kewensis*. He had the assistance of Banks's librarians, Jonas Dryander and Robert Brown. Brown continued to help and advise, and frequently visited Kew after his appointment in 1805 as Keeper of Botany at the British Museum. The second edition of *Hortus Kewensis* appeared in five volumes between 1810 and 1813 in a print run of 1,250 copies, and in 1814 gardeners were offered a cheaper and more portable edition, an *Epitome*.[46] In 1817, when Aiton was starting to compile a revised edition of the *Epitome*, which took much time over the years but was never published, he produced his only other recorded publication, a paper for the RHS on the 'Cultivation of Winter Cucumbers' for which, and 'for his polite and obliging attention to the Society and to its officers at all times', he received the Society's Silver Medal.[47]

By 1813 there had been no increase in the amounts payable under the contracts of the Royal Gardeners since they had been established, the oldest going back to 1784 and the latest to 1801. These were outside the responsibility of the Board of Green Cloth and were under the old 'contract' arrangement. While inflation was slight compared with the present day, costs had materially increased as a consequence of the Napoleonic war, and William Townsend Aiton, Wm. Padley and John Townsend Aiton, His Majesty's Gardeners at Kensington, Kew, Hampton Court and Windsor, 'severally represented ... the inadequacy of the means allotted by their respective contracts for the maintenance of the Gardens under their management'.

On 25 January 1813 the Master of the Household – now a Mr G.Stone – put the Gardeners' detailed proposals for the consideration of the Lords Commissioners of His Majesty's Treasury, recommending their acceptance.[48] The Treasury concurred, establishing an increase in these contract amounts for the four gardens together from £7,039 15s 10d to £8,626 5s 11d – an increase of 22.5%, which came into force almost immediately.[49]

It may be that these increases drew the attention of the Treasury to the Royal Gardens, as they were followed by a request to the Lord Steward on 5 July 1816, as part of a larger review of the Lord Steward's department, to transmit to their lordships a list of the several Royal Gardens. This specified the particular nature of the Gardens, and 'the purposes and objects for which they are kept up, together with an account of the Actual Expense of each garden incurred in the [Lord Steward's] Department in the last seven years; and ... in what manner and for whose Benefit the surplus produce of those gardens has been disposed of '.[50]

The Master of the Household supported the Aitons' garden arrangements, and there is no sign of any immediate comment from the Treasury. However, as from the beginning of 1816, the long established contract system whereby a contract price was set for each garden, and the 'Contractor' gardener met all expenses from the figure set, was replaced by the appointment of a 'Controller' in the Lord Steward's Department at £500 p.a. who seems to have paid the expenses of all the gardens as submitted by the head gardeners. A professional valuation of Garden Implements and Stock of the Royal Gardens at Kensington, Kew, Windsor, Cumberland Lodge and Hampton Court upon the transfer on 5 April 1817 totalled £1,574 9s, of which the Aitons accounted for £1,023 16s 6d. It is doubtful that this measure improved efficiency, but it must have made life easier for Aiton.

Aiton was much involved in finding men suitable for plant hunting overseas, in which he worked with Banks who made the final selection. Among those plant hunting in Aiton's time were Francis Masson, George Caley, Peter Good, William Kerr, James Wiles, W.Roxburgh, J.F.von Jaquin, Alan Cunningham, James Bowie, James Hooper, David Lockhart, A.P.Hove and Archibald Menzies. The war with France hindered such expeditions, but from Kew's point of view this was somewhat offset by captures from the French. However, in May 1814 when hostilities had ceased Aiton wrote to Banks proposing a resumption of overseas collecting, saying he had suitable men of sound principles and invaluable zeal and suggesting that the proposal be put to the Treasury.[51] Later that year following an approach by Banks to the Treasury, Bowie and Cunningham were dispatched to South Africa and Brazil, and Cunningham later to Australia and New Zealand.[52] An important part of Aiton's time must have been taken up in seeing to the administration of the expeditions and the handling of the resulting collections.

The years 1815 to 1820 saw things quieten down at Kew, and Aiton was increasingly in demand elsewhere. Banks paid his last visit to Kew in 1819; he died on 19 June the following year. The Duke of Kent died on 23 January 1820 and King George III on 25 October, being succeeded by George IV who had acted as Prince Regent for nearly ten years.

Chapter 4: The Landscape Widens

With George IV as king, a new era began for Aiton. As Roy Strong has observed, 'George IV's garden making would be dominated by two people: the architect John Nash and the Royal Gardener William Townsend Aiton who were to carry through all his main creations.'[53]

As a young man Aiton had wished to be a landscape gardener and garden designer, but when his father died in 1793 he had immediately to take over the gardens at Kew. Landscape gardening had to be forgotten. Now the opportunity came at the age of 54. He was to work with the King's architects – Repton, Nash, Wyatville and Blore. His contribution enabled them to put their ideas into practice, and he was also able to exercise his own skills in garden design.

To leave Aiton more time to attend the King, John Smith, who had come from the Edinburgh Botanic Garden, was transferred to Kew from Kensington Palace in 1822 and promoted to foreman in the following year, holding that position until appointed Curator in 1841. In his *History of the Royal Gardens at Kew*, written after his retirement in 1864 but never published, Smith gives these glimpses of Aiton at work.

> It was Mr Aiton's custom to drive in a gig almost daily from Kew to Windsor, for if for any inadvertent reason he was prevented for two or three days, a mounted dragoon carrying a message from the King was sure to be seen early in the morning at his house in Kew... He attended George IV at Windsor almost daily for many years leaving little time for the *Epitome* ... For two or three years he made a rule of spending two or three hours in his garden office every night assisted by his amanuensis Richard Cunningham and a young gardener as copyist...[54]

Nash and Aiton were then creating the new gardens at Royal Lodge, which the King had adopted as his residence at Windsor.

They also worked together on the Royal Gardens at Brighton, Buckingham Palace (then known as the Queen's House) and St James's Park. Nash was no horticulturalist and needed the assistance of Aiton in creating what is now regarded as the Regency Gardening Style, with the restorations in St James's Park, and of the gardens of the Brighton Royal Pavilion, using Aiton's original plant lists.[55]

At Buckingham Palace Aiton swept away Wise's formal gardens established a century before. 'In place of the old parterres, avenues and flower beds, a new terrace the length of the garden front of Nash's building, led down to a huge sweep of lawn. Beyond Aiton joined the existing two ponds together and enlarged them into the present lake, removing the excavated earth to form the mound on the south-west side of the gardens.'[56] He was also involved at Windsor with Sir Jeffrey Wyatville where he designed the East Terrace garden, which remained almost unchanged until 1953 when it was replaced by a rose garden.[57]

A little light on his work with the King in developing Virginia Water and its surroundings comes in a series of anecdotes in the *Gardeners' Chronicle* in 1874 from a Mr Morris who had worked as a labourer on the Royal Estates at Windsor. 'The King with the Marchioness of Conningham at his side desired Mr Aiton to ride on horseback, as he always did when out with the King, to a place in the Park called Belvedere where the King wished to give directions for cutting down some trees.' Here Mr Morris gives an example of how things were done: 'Now all this was laid out by Thomson [a trainee, later head gardener at Syon House] under the direction of Mr Nitchell [head gardener at Royal Lodge], from plans prepared by Mr Aiton. I helped to dig the holes to receive the trees after they were brought from the Duke of Marlborough's sale at Whiteknights near Reading. Mr Aiton took [Thomson] to Whiteknights some days before the sale, and marked the lots for him to purchase.'[58]

While Aiton was working on the King's many projects he still had responsibility for Kew's Botanic and Pleasure Gardens. Being a Kew resident, and also the Royal Gardener at Kew, he had much to do with the enclosure of Kew Green and the riverside meadows, and the redrawing of boundaries under the 1824 Enclosure Act. He was in a difficult position, particularly as he, in common with other well-to-do inhabitants, stood to gain from enclosures. It appears to have fallen to him to represent the Crown to the Vestry. In 1822, for example, he conveyed to the Vestry 'His Majesty's gracious intention to present an Organ and build a gallery for its reception' in St Anne's church on Kew Green. In return the Vestry asked Aiton to convey to His Majesty their 'humble and dutiful thanks'.[59]

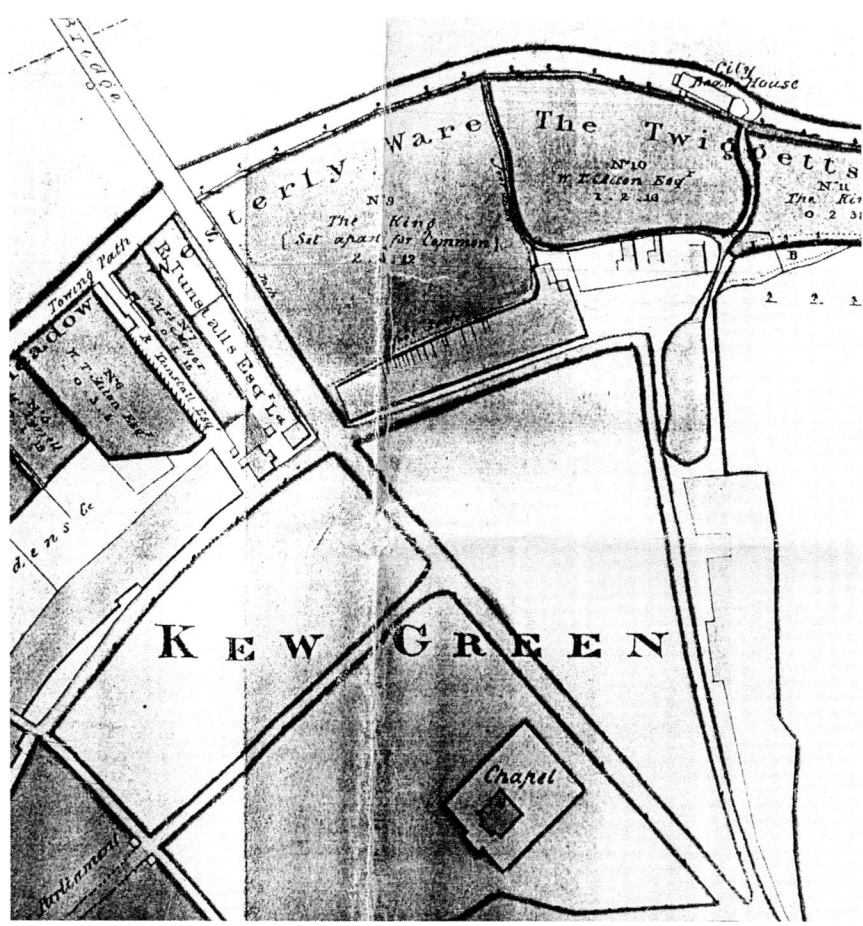

The Enclosure Map of Kew Green, showing the two substantial areas allocated to W.T.Aiton Esq

George IV is said never to have shown much affection for Kew, and there is no indication that he showed any wish to encourage the Botanic Garden, where Aiton maintained the status quo. Aiton was under pressure to supply plants from the Royal Gardens to nurserymen but, following the policy established under George III with Sir Joseph Banks, he zealously guarded them as the King's property, though he was generous to other botanic gardens. Later he would be criticised for being too niggardly, and it may have been in this connection that he was described by a later writer as a 'fanatic'.[60] Young gardeners were being bribed to steal from the gardens and in 1824 Aiton arranged for a case to be brought against Robert Sweet of Colville's Nursery for receiving stolen plants. Sweet, who was a well-known and popular nurseryman, was acquitted – on a technicality according to Smith. Smith also refers to the jealousies of nurserymen and others, which were perhaps to be expected.

In 1821 the Royal Horticultural Society leased a 33-acre site in Chiswick from the Duke of Devonshire in a new venture to have its own gardens. The venture had the backing of horticulturalists, and it was said that it 'rapidly usurped the prominent position in collecting circles that Kew had held until the death of Banks'.[61] Kew meanwhile, though Royal and with an unrivalled reputation, was a private garden in which the owners had almost lost interest and its head gardener was busy working elsewhere for his Royal master.

In 1826/7 a German garden enthusiast Prince Puckler-Muskau, who was in England visiting famous British gardens, confirmed what might be expected at Kew in the circumstances: 'Kew ... unquestionably possesses the most complete collection of exotic plants in Europe. The Park has a great advantage in its beautiful situation on the Thames, but is in general rather neglected.'[62] Other visitors made similar comments.[63]

Aiton was, however, doing what his employer wanted at Kew and elsewhere. In Kensington, for example, five new lodges were erected to his design in 1827.[64] In October he was designated 'Director General of His Majesties Gardens'.[65] A little later, no doubt to reduce the pressure on Aiton, his brother John Townsend Aiton was appointed 'Deputy

Director General' by Warrant dated 2 July 1829 at a salary of £700 p.a.[66]

It seems that the King added one scheme after another to Aiton's 'portfolio' and Aiton accepted everything the King asked him to do. With his upbringing he could never say 'No' to a task presented to him by the King; and it must have been all too easy for the King to turn to Aiton to manage any new scheme that took his fancy. One has the feeling that in the end Aiton found it had become too much: his appointment as Director General with his brother as Deputy Director General was offered as a solution, but the addition of an overall responsibility for all Royal Gardens was hardly an easing of the load.

When George IV died in 1830, William IV reversed a number of his brother's actions, including the return to Kew Green of some 100 yards which had been added to the grounds of Kew Palace. He is said to have had an affection for Kew but he gave no greater support than his predecessor to the Botanic Garden other than finding a home at Kew for one of Nash's conservatories no longer required at Buckingham Palace.

It seems that the reign of the new monarch may have started inauspiciously for Aiton with a problem left over from the reign of George IV. It had been the custom for Aiton to carry out 'ground and plantation works of the King's own ordering and daily inspection' at Royal Lodge; the work was organised and paid for by Aiton and the expense refunded by Treasury grant. In May 1828 however, the Treasury had for whatever reason suspended the grants to meet the cost of these works, leaving Aiton in a dilemma. On 29 May 1830 he wrote to Sir William Knighton, Keeper of the Privy Purse, asking advice on whom he should approach to have his expenses refunded.[67] Before anything was settled, the King died, and Aiton approached the Duke of Wellington by letter dated July 1830 putting his case.[68] His letter explained that following the cessation of the Treasury grants to meet his expenses, the King and Lord Harcourt, the Deputy Ranger, authorised timber in Windsor Great Park to be cut down to defray these costs, and that when Sir William Knighton heard of it he consulted the Marquis of Hertford, who countermanded the

One of John Nash's conservatories, here seen at Buckingham Palace, was transferred to Kew in 1836. The lake in the foreground was designed by Aiton.

authorisation on the grounds that he feared the action would be 'injurious to the picturesqueness of the Park'.

We do not know how the dilemma was resolved, but it is hard to believe that it was settled without the knowledge of William IV. The episode could conceivably have been the trigger for his action, soon after coming to the throne, to abolish the post of Director General and remove from William Townsend Aiton responsibility for the Royal Gardens other than Richmond and Kew. The posts of Deputy Director General and of Controller were abolished at the same time. From now on the head gardener for each garden became directly responsible to the Board of Green Cloth.

William IV, in contrast to George IV, was little interested in gardens, and a garden 'supremo' was to him unnecessary. It is probably fair to say that in his view all that was needed was for each Royal Garden to be looked after by having a gardener locally in charge. He wavered from this at Windsor after two years when Ingram, who previously had been gardener at Royal Lodge, was put in charge of all the five gardens on the Windsor estate.

Aiton, now 64, was given a 'retirement salary', which continued for the rest of his life, of £1,000 p.a. plus his house, coals and a paddock − a generous arrangement, which he may have been content to accept. It was a reduction from his previous salary of £1,400, but with reduced responsibilities. If William IV, as has been said, disliked Aiton, he treated him kindly.

The King left him in charge of the continuing reorganisation of the gardens of Buckingham Palace. (Edward Blore had been commissioned to complete alterations to the house.) This reorganisation, which had started with Aiton and Nash working together, had continued for some years funded by the Office of Woods and Forests which had to claim Aiton's costs from the Treasury. It appears that by 1830 this had gone on so long that Woods and Forests attempted to pass the costs on to the Lord Steward, but the Treasury ruled that the costs should be met from funds under the management of Woods and Forests 'until the Palace is fit for HM occupation'.[69] Aiton's expenses at Buckingham Palace would continue into the reign of Queen Victoria − in December 1837 his advice was quoted to justify the specification of the hot-water apparatus to be installed in the greenhouses and he was asked to advise on the treatment of boundary trees objected to by the Trustees of the Grosvenor district (the Grosvenor Estate).[70]

In 1832 when Kensington Palace came into use for the Duchess of Kent and Princess Victoria, and for the Duke of Sussex, its gardens were in such condition that the Treasury had sanctioned the works necessary for restoring them to a more ornamental condition and for keeping them up in a manner similar to the pleasure gardens in St James's Park, Hyde Park and Regent's Park. For want of funds they had for many years been left without improvement, and it was apparent that trees and plantations had become so overgrown that nothing could be done until skilful clearance and thinning had been undertaken. The Board of Woods and Forests asked Aiton to undertake the work to ensure the improvement of the plantations and the general appearance of the grounds. This he did to everyone's satisfaction. It was an extensive extra duty in grounds outside his area of management, and in 1835 Woods and Forests approached the Treasury for permission to make him a gratuity of £200, pointing out that he had necessarily incurred travelling and other incidental expenses, and spent a considerable portion of his time carefully selecting such items as seemed to him proper for taking down, which he afterwards prepared for auction realising 'upwards of £5,000'. It was also to recognise 'the attention with which he has met the requests of the Board on this and former similar occasions, in addition to the usual duties of his own situation'. The Treasury considered that a grant equivalent to £50 p.a. for the three years in which he had given these services was appropriate, and were pleased to authorise £150.[71]

William Forsyth Jnr, one of Aiton's oldest friends and a principal London seedsman, died in 1835, leaving a library described as 'one of the most extensive private libraries of horticultural literature, perhaps ever collected'.[72] The library was auctioned at his death by Sotheby's, when a number of items were bought by Aiton to appear again when Aiton's library in turn was auctioned in 1851 after his death. Forsyth also left 'miniature paintings of Mr Aiton, Mr Robert Gray and my father to Mr Aiton my Executor as a memento of the friendship which has always existed between our respective families'. (The precise whereabouts of these miniatures is not known, but there are miniatures of William Aiton in the Fitzwilliam and Victoria and Albert Museums, and there is at least one miniature of William Aiton by Engleheart in private hands.)

By 1838 there had for some years been public criticism of the Royal Gardens, including Kew, reaching a crescendo in 1837/8 in a series of articles in the *Gardeners' Gazette*, and letters to *The Times*. At the same time there was Treasury pressure to reduce the costs of the Royal Establishment, and the Royal Gardens became a target.

The extent of the gardens can be illustrated by the manning in the March Quarter 1834, as shown in the Royal Garden Bills.[73] (The Buckingham Palace Gardens came under Woods and Forests.)

Kew: (William T.Aiton at a salary of £1000 p.a.)
Kitchen and Forcing Grounds – a foreman, two men in charge of hot houses, vegetable man, watchman, and six labourers.
Botanic Gardens – a foreman (John Smith), an office man, a collector of seeds, watchman, fireman, twenty-one labourers.

Kensington : (John T.Aiton at a salary of £450 p.a.)
Forcing Ground – a foreman, two labourers and three boys.
Kitchen Garden – a foreman, melon ground man, twelve labourers and a boy.
Palace Garden – a foreman with a labourer.

Windsor: (J.Ingram at a salary of £150 p.a. for Windsor and Cumberland Lodge.)
Six separate gardens: Maestricht, Frogmore, Cumberland Lodge, King's Lodge, Cranbourne and the Royal Gardens and slopes at Windsor Castle. Each had its own foreman and between them, though quite separately, they employed thirty-eight gardeners of various categories – seven attending the Terrace on Sundays.

Brighton: a foreman and three labourers.

Hampton Court: (A.Turrell at £150 p.a.)
Melon ground and kitchen garden – a foreman each, with a total of nineteen labourers including three for the private garden.

It is little wonder that the Treasury questioned the need for such expense and now called for a review of these Royal Gardens. On 30 January 1838 a Treasury Committee, under the Earl of Surrey, Lord Steward, with two MPs, Edward Ellice and Robert Gordon, was appointed: 'for the purpose of enquiry into the superintendence, management and expenditure of the Royal Gardens and of reporting their opinion'.[74]

Dr John Lindley, Professor of Botany at University College London and Assistant Secretary of the Royal Horticultural Society, was asked to form a working party, with John Wilson, gardener to the Earl of Surrey, and Joseph Paxton, gardener to the Duke of Devonshire. It took Lindley less than six weeks of the worst of winter weather to draw up a comprehensive report and recommendations, in the preparation of which the working party visited all the gardens, took recorded evidence and asked for and obtained detailed written information on each. His report was adopted by the Committee on 10 March.

One of the criticisms was that there was no coordination, nor even communication, between the various Royal Gardens. Aiton's evidence as quoted was that 'in his opinion the Gardens have suffered injury for want of a system of control.'[75]

It was eight years since Aiton, as Director General, had last had overall responsibility. Now he answered for Kew alone, and Kew came in for particular criticism. Much of the explanation was lack of money – budget cuts had reduced expenditure from an annual average of £1900 in 1824/27 to £1460 in 1828/31 and to £1277 in 1832/36, at a time of rising costs.[76] Royalty, whose garden it was, were not prepared to support Aiton, and Kew had become a prime target for economy and for criticism. With Aiton now 70, and without support, it is not surprising that Kew suffered and was threatened with extinction.

Aiton had tried in 1831 to obtain the transfer of some acres from the pleasure grounds to enlarge the Arboretum, but nobody was interested.[77] He was a functionary – and must have been a good one – in the sense that he was paid to work for Royalty in a 'private capacity' to supervise the very extensive Royal Gardens, but not to initiate policy on garden development. His appointment as Director General in 1828 might have implied a wider role, but that appointment lasted less than two years and by then he was too old and tired for a new vision.

There was a delay of two years while the report, and in particular the future of Kew, were debated behind the scenes, before the Committee's Report relating to Kew was presented to Parliament on 4 May 1840, and Lindley's recommendations eight days later. On 25 June the Treasury sanctioned the transfer of the Botanic Gardens, from the Lord Steward's Department to Woods and Forests, and the Botanic Gardens at Kew were established as a National Institution with a scientific brief – no longer part of the Royal Establishment. Four days later the Prime Minister and Lord Duncannon, chairman of Woods and Forests, approved the appointment of Sir William Hooker as the new Director.[78]

The Kitchen Garden, the grounds of Kew Palace and the Queen's Cottage were to be left with the Lord Steward's Department with Aiton in charge. He also continued, under the auspices of Woods and Forests, to be involved with the gardens at Buckingham Palace. However, the conflicting views on the appropriate future for Kew which had delayed the submission of the Report to Parliament were still unresolved, and it was not until 23 May 1841 that Aiton was notified by the Commissioners of Woods and Forests of the appointment of Hooker as Director. He immediately wrote to Hooker welcoming the appointment in view of his 'long desire of resignation' and invited him to his house.[79]

It would be interesting to know how Aiton regarded the next eight years until his death. He knew well that much needed to be done at Kew, and one hopes it was with satisfaction, though perhaps with envy, that he saw four acres of the Pleasure Gardens near the Orangery taken to add to the Botanic Garden, and in 1843 a further 45 acres granted by the Queen to extend the Botanic Garden and provide extra space for the Arboretum and to provide a site for the Palm House. One would hope he welcomed the vigorous, and well supported, development by a younger man of what had so long been his responsibility. The last stages soon followed when, first in 1845 he relinquished to Hooker the management of the Pleasure Grounds, an extensive area of approaching 200 acres, and in 1846, then aged 80, his last charge, the Kitchen Garden, until then retained for the private use of the Crown.[80]

His remaining sister had died in May 1848 and for the first time in his life he had none of his family living with him. His time was increasingly spent at his brother's house at Palace Gate, Kensington, where he died on 9 October 1849. Until then, we are told, 'He enjoyed in general good health and spirits notwithstanding that his pulse seldom reached 50.'[81]

His will was proved in the sum of around £7,000 on 22 November 1849 by his joint executors, his brother John Townsend Aiton and William Atwell Smith, who shared the estate subject to a few minor legacies.[82] Both of the Aiton brothers appointed Atwell Smith as executor and a major beneficiary at their death. They had no family of their own and their high regard for Atwell Smith is unexplained. Records show that a William Atwell Smith was born in 1798 and christened at St Marylebone, second of a family of four children born at roughly two year intervals, all of them reasonably well to do – a brother of substance having considerable family property, and two sisters. Many years later, John Smith referred to him as believed to be the natural son of William Aiton. From the context it is clear that he meant William Townsend Aiton.

John Townsend Aiton had no family and when he died on 4 July 1851, aged 74, William Atwell Smith as executor and residuary legatee offered John's library and herbarium of 250 items to Kew, including his brother William's books and specimens. Lord Seymour, First Commissioner of Works and Public Buildings and Woods and Forests, refused the offer, and they were sold at auction, along with John Aiton's fine collection of pictures and objets d'art.

In view of their Royal service of nearly a century in a period of historic garden development, it was a tragedy that nearly all the Aitons' private and professional papers were inexplicably destroyed by John shortly before his death. William Atwell Smith gave to Kew such documents and papers relating to the Royal Gardens as had survived, including some 2,000 plant drawings which William had had made over the years, and 13 volumes of plant records in rough calf-leather bindings, together with the portrait of William Aiton. It was sad too that there was no one to inherit their possessions and care for their memory, though William Atwell Smith, whatever his connection, did his best.

Acknowledgements

I express my most sincere thanks to all who have helped in collecting the information on which this article is based.

In particular, I thank the Library of the Royal Botanic Gardens (RBG), for their generous support and for giving a home to my research notes on the Aitons. I am also indebted to the expertise of The National Archives (TNA), the Duchy of Cornwall Archives (DCA), Surrey History Centre (SHC), the Royal Horticultural Society (RHS), Kensington Record Office, the British Library Department of Manuscripts, Richmond Local Studies Library, the Botany Library and Picture Library of the Natural History Museum, the Linnean Society Library, the Greater London Record Office, Chiswick Library Local Studies Department, and the Victoria and Albert National Art Library.

The references from the Royal Archives (RA) are included by gracious permission of her Majesty the Queen.

I have also benefited from the background provided by articles published in the *Journal of the Garden History Society (GHSJ)*, and by many books, most particularly the following:

Aiton, William, *An Inquiry into the Origin, Pedigree, & History of the Family, or Clan, of Aitons in Scotland* (Hamilton, 1830)
Allan, M, *The Hookers of Kew* (Michael Joseph, 1967)
Batey, Mavis, *Regency Gardens* (Shire, 1995)
Desmond, Ray, *Kew, The History of the Royal Botanic Gardens* (Harvill Press, 1995)
Fletcher, H.R., *The Story of the RHS 1804-1968* (OUP, 1969)
Hedley, Olwen, *Queen Charlotte* (John Murray, 1975)
Jacques, David, *Georgian Gardens: the Reign of Nature* (Batsford, 1983)
Mabey, R, *The Flowering of Kew* (Ebury Press, 1988)
Plumtre, George, *Royal Gardens* (Monacelli, 2005)
Roberts, Jane, *Royal Landscape, the Gardens and Parks of Windsor* (Yale, 1997)
Strong, Roy, *Royal Gardens* (London: BBC, 1992)

Notes and Sources

[1] Aiton pp 38-40
[2] DCA Princess Augusta's Household Accounts vol 43(1) p 40
[3] John Smith, *History of the Royal Gardens, Kew* , p 481
[4] DCA Princess Augusta's Household Accounts vol 59 pp 42-3
[5] Desmond p 41
[6] Desmond p 41
[7] Desmond p 85
[8] Desmond p 38
[9] British Library MSS Banks Correspondence 33.977 f 120
[10] TNA LS/3/107 p 24
[11] TNA T/54/45 f 20
[12] TNA WORK 275/65
[13] Desmond p 36
[14] *Gentleman's Magazine* – 6 May 1793
[16] J.E.Smith, *Memoir and Correspondence*, vol 2, p58
[16] F. McNko Bladon ed., *The Diaries of Colonel The Hon. Robert Fulke Greville,* (John Lane The Bodley Head, 1930)
[17] Mabey p 6
[18] R. Brown, British Library MSS 32441 p 448
[19] Roberts p 67
[20] Desmond p 97
[21] Desmond p 98
[22] TNA LS 10/5
[23] TNA LS 13/107 p 39
[24] TNA LS 13/107 p 39
[25] TNA LS 13/107 pp 43-8 and 50
[26] TNA LS 10/4 pp 11-27
[27] Hedley p 227
[28] TNA LS 10/8 pp 435 & 436
[29] TNA LS 10/4 pp 136-7
[30] TNA LS 10/3 p 39
[31] TNA LS 10/3 pp 48-56
[32] TNA WO13 4050
[33] TNA WO13 4050
[34] Aiton to Banks, Dawson Turner Correspondence 14 pp 120-6
[35] Fletcher p 21
[36] British Library MSS 32441
[37] TNA LS 10/3
[38] Smith Corr. 1. 127 Linnean Soc.
[39] British Library MSS 33981 f 261
[40] TNA LS 10/3 p 63
[41] TNA WORK 19/16/2
[42] TNA LS 10/3 pp 80 & 96; LS 11/1 p 328

[43] TNA LS 10/7 p 220
[44] TNA LS 13/265/179
[45] TNA WORK 6/26
[46] Desmond p 201
[47] RHS Council Minutes 21.1.1817
[48] TNA LS 10/3 pp 68-71
[49] TNA LS 10/9
[50] TNA LS 11/1 pp 324-38
[51] British Library MSS 33982 p 60
[52] Banks to Harrison - Sept 1814
[53] Strong, p 81
[54] John Smith, *History of the Royal Gardens, Kew* pp 485 & 280
[55] Batey p 85
[56] Plumtre p 169
[57] Roberts p 173
[58] Payments to I.Nitchell and J.Morris appear in the Garden Bills at King's Lodge, Windsor in 1834. See TNA LS 11/19 p 78
[59] SHC Kew Vestry Minutes - 22 May 1822
[60] Allan p 58
[61] Jacques p 190
[62] Pucklers Progress, 1987
[63] Desmond p.132
[64] TNA WORK 4/21, pp 218, 224, 250
[65] RA 24208
[66] TNA T 90/190 - Royal Garden Enquiry 1838
[67] RA 34645
[68] RA 34646
[69] TNA WORK 19/10/4 26 Jan. 1830
[70] TNA WORK 19/10/4 1and 20 Dec. 1837
[71] TNA T/I 3903 26 June 1835
[72] David Jacques GHSJ Vol24/1 pp 58-65
[73] TNA LS 11/19
[74] TNA T90/189
[75] 1838 Report on Royal Gardens p 83
[76] Lindley Report
[77] TNA T/I 3963 and Desmond p 172
[78] TNA LS 11/25 and Desmond p 149
[79] Letters to Hooker, RBG
[80] Desmond p 367
[81] Linnean Society Proceedings 1851
[82] TNA PROB 11/2102